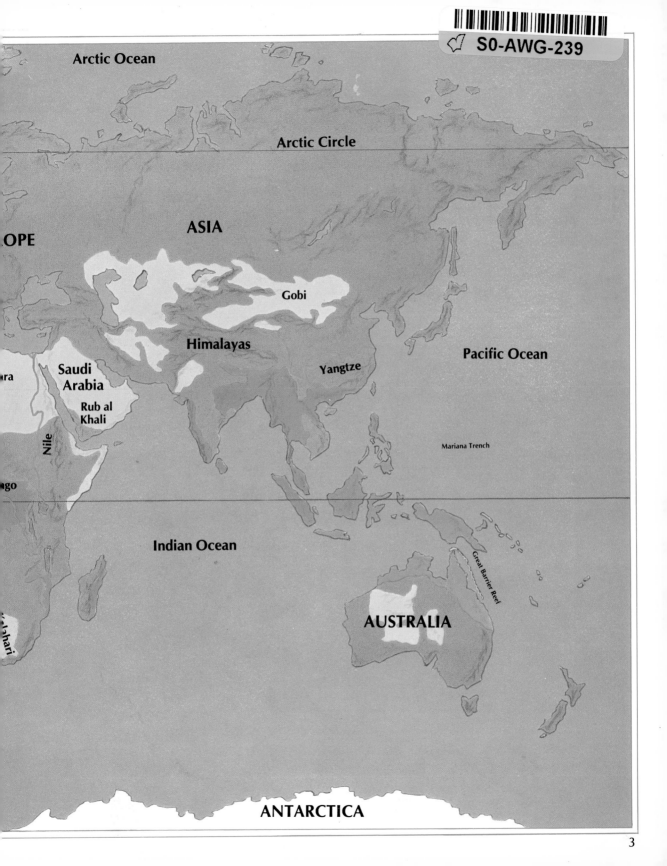

Arctic Ocean

Arctic Circle

ASIA

OPE

Gobi

Himalayas

Saudi
Arabia

ra

Rub al
Khali

Yangtze

Pacific Ocean

Nile

Mariana Trench

go

Indian Ocean

Great Barrier Reef

AUSTRALIA

hari

ANTARCTICA

Illustrators
Denise Finney pages 14-15, 16-17
Barbara Firth pages 10-11
Nick Hardcastle pages 18-19, 22-23
Stephen Kyte pages 26-27, 28-29
Mark Longworth end sheets,
pages 24-25
Deirdre Morgan pages 8-9
Tom Stimpson cover, pages 12-13
Gillian Tomblin title page,
pages 6-7, 20-21

Designer Pat Butterworth

First published 1984 by Walker Books Ltd,
17-19 Hanway House, Hanway Place,
London W1P 9DL

© 1984 Walker Books Ltd

First printed 1984
Printed and bound in Spain
by Artes Graficas Toledo, S.A. DL-TO-157-84

British Library Cataloguing in Publication Data
Boase, Wendy
Earth traveller. – (Young explorers; 2)
1. Earth – Juvenile literature
I. Title II. Series
550   QE29
ISBN 0-7445-0111-3

Contents

In this book:

mm	=	millimetres
cm	=	centimetres
m	=	metres
km	=	kilometres
sq	=	square
°C	=	degrees Centigrade
%	=	percentage

To read the answer to a quiz,
hold a mirror at the right-
hand side of the words.

EARTH TRAVELLER

By Wendy Boase
Consultant Dr John Griffiths

WALKER BOOKS
LONDON

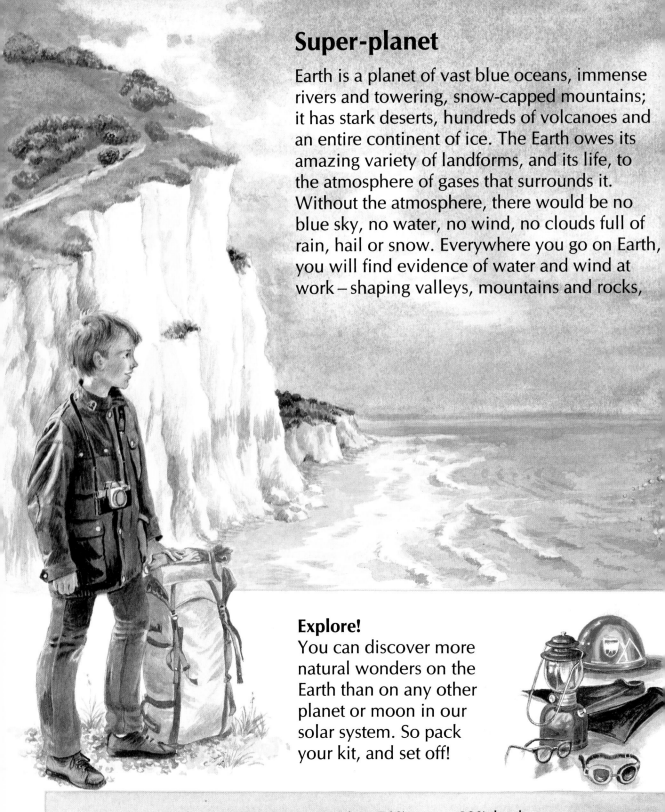

Super-planet

Earth is a planet of vast blue oceans, immense rivers and towering, snow-capped mountains; it has stark deserts, hundreds of volcanoes and an entire continent of ice. The Earth owes its amazing variety of landforms, and its life, to the atmosphere of gases that surrounds it. Without the atmosphere, there would be no blue sky, no water, no wind, no clouds full of rain, hail or snow. Everywhere you go on Earth, you will find evidence of water and wind at work – shaping valleys, mountains and rocks,

Explore!
You can discover more natural wonders on the Earth than on any other planet or moon in our solar system. So pack your kit, and set off!

.................Earth's area 510,066,000 sq km; 71% water, 29% land........................

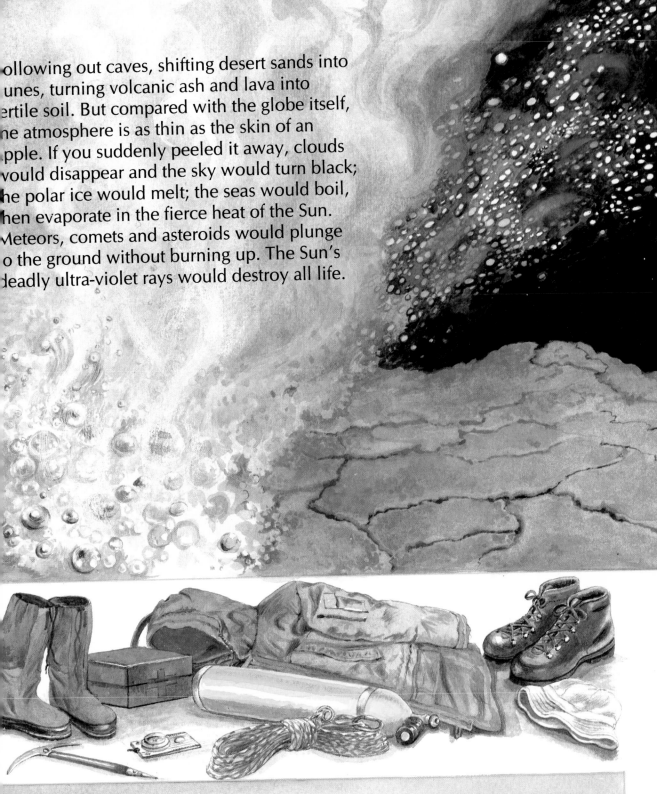

ollowing out caves, shifting desert sands into
unes, turning volcanic ash and lava into
ertile soil. But compared with the globe itself,
ne atmosphere is as thin as the skin of an
pple. If you suddenly peeled it away, clouds
vould disappear and the sky would turn black;
he polar ice would melt; the seas would boil,
hen evaporate in the fierce heat of the Sun.
Meteors, comets and asteroids would plunge
o the ground without burning up. The Sun's
deadly ultra-violet rays would destroy all life.

ircumference at Equator 40,000 km… atmosphere about 50km thick……………………

Dive!

Slip on a mask, grip the air hose in your mouth, and dive! You are in a watery world that covers nearly three-quarters of our planet. Suddenly you feel weightless; you glide like a bird, powered only by your arms and flippered feet. Ten metres down in the Caribbean Sea, you sink gently on to a reef. Deep, sandy gullies wind through thick forests of living coral. Fish dart away from the rising bubbles of your exhaled air. Sea-water is rich in life, whether it is a shallow tropical sea like this, the dark depths of the Pacific Ocean, or the icy water of the Arctic.

Quiz
Why would a grape be a successful deep-sea diver?

Answer
A grape consists mostly of water, so deep-sea pressure would not crush it.

.... Biggest ocean, Pacific (166,241,000 sq km)..............deepest part, Mariana Trenc

Dangerous diving
Deep water can kill you. Its coldness can cause you to black out. Its weight compresses (or squeezes up) the air in your ears, nose and lungs, crushing your body. A whale's body tissue consists mostly of water, which can't be compressed as air can. Whales dive to nearly 2km, a depth where you need a pressure suit.

Tiny builders
Billions of sea animals called polyps create coral. The skeletons and hard shells of dead polyps build the base. Live polyps, housed in their shells, form the top layer. The Great Barrier Reef, off Australia, has 350 varieties of coral.

cific Ocean (10,915 m)............... longest reef, Great Barrier Reef (2,000 km)..............

Desert survival

Walking into a desert is as awesome as diving deep into an ocean, and just as dangerous. In a desert, you could die in 48 hours if you had no shelter or water. Not all deserts are sandy. Some are rocky or stony, and others have large areas of salt or even ice.

Nor are all deserts hot. What they have in common is very little rain. The Gobi in Asia is a very cold, dry desert with less than 100 mm of rain a year. Animals and plants manage to survive in deserts. So can you, by knowing a few special tricks.

In the hot **Sahara Desert,** which covers one-third of Africa, there are few oases. Trust your camel to find one if it's a few kilometres away. Camels can sense water that is too distant to see.

The **Atacama** in South America is a cold desert, and the world's driest. But you could collect the water in sea fog. Stretch some nylon threads across a frame, and wait for beads of moisture to form on them.

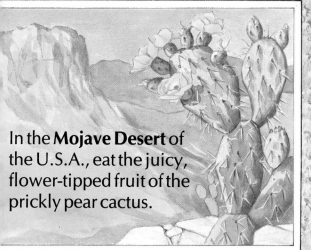

In the **Mojave Desert** of the U.S.A., eat the juicy, flower-tipped fruit of the prickly pear cactus.

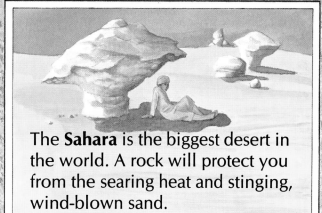

The **Sahara** is the biggest desert in the world. A rock will protect you from the searing heat and stinging, wind-blown sand.

The **Kalahari** in southern Africa is a semi-desert with underground water. Suck the water up through a reed, as the local Bushmen do.

On the edge of the **Australian Desert,** pierce the trunk of a baobab tree and drink the water stored in it.

The **Rub al Khali** in Saudi Arabia is a 'sea' of arid dunes and salt flats. You could milk your camel to quench your thirst.

In the **Namib Desert** of south-west Africa, probe dried-up streams for the moist, edible roots of water-lilies.

Polar trek

The ice glitters beneath a cloudless blue sky. Your warm breath freezes instantly into millions of rainbow-coloured crystals. This is the Antarctic, a frozen continent where so little rain or snow falls that it is as much a desert as the Sahara. The temperature is −50°C, but on a bright day like this near the South Pole, you can be badly sunburned by ultra-violet rays.

Quiz
Could you eat a month-old cup-cake in Antarctica?

Answer
Yes. It would stay fresh in the pure, germ-free air.

..........Coldest continent, Antarctica; lowest temperature −88.3°C........... biggest iceb

Light, passing through layers of warm and cold air, causes mirages which trick your eyes. You might see ships or mountains floating upside down in the sky, or see the Sun rise and set many times in one day. The Antarctic air is the purest and driest on Earth; there is no damp air or pollution to rust metal, and no germs or bacteria to rot meat or make bread mouldy.

South to north
The Antarctic is an icy land surrounded by sea. Penguins and many other animals live in the ocean, but there is little life on the land. The Arctic, near the North Pole, is an icy sea surrounded by land. Polar bears, reindeer and foxes live on the land within the Arctic Circle. Even flowers and small trees grow there.

ger than Belgium), Antarctica… ………… smallest ocean, Arctic (9,485,000 sq km)……….

Jungle walk

Beneath the towering jungle trees, it is hot, dark and damp. Your shirt sticks to you, your hair feels limp. There is no greater contrast to the frozen Antarctic. Jungles teem with life – over half of all the animals and plants on Earth live in these hot, wet tropical forests near the Equator.

At midday, thunder cracks; lightning splits the sky. The first raindrops fall, like large silver coins. Suddenly the rain is pounding down, soaking your clothes. Mould will grow on them if you don't find a sunny river bank or clearing. In the Amazon jungle, just 10% of sunlight reaches the ground, so there is no thick undergrowth. You need a machete only where a tree has crashed under the weight of plants climbing up it to reach the light.

.... Biggest jungle, the Amazon, South America (10 times the size of France).

You Tarzan

Like Tarzan, you could eat fish, wild bananas, potatoes and avocadoes. But you must know your lianas before you go swinging in the jungle. These rope-like vines can grow up to 180 m. Many have sharp hooks and claws, and others contain poisons.

Quiz
Why don't you need to wear sunglasses in a jungle?

Answer
It isn't sunny on the jungle floor. Tall trees keep out light.

River ride

Paddling furiously through rapids on the Amazon River, not far from its source, you dodge vicious boulders, ride the crests of waves, dip low in the churning foam. The torrent rages ahead, smashing against rocks with a terrifying force. A swift river like this carries big stones with it. They grind against the riverbed and the banks, helping to wear down rocks and hills.

A slow river, such as the Mississippi in the U.S.A. or the Yangtze in China, shapes the land by depositing fine silt and gravel along its winding course. The Amazon, too, slows down as it winds through the area of flat jungle towards the sea. Every day, it pours out one-fifth of all the river-water on Earth, muddying the Atlantic for hundreds of kilometres out to sea.

.. River with greatest flow, Amazon, South America........................ longest river, Nil

Action underground
More fresh water exists below ground than above. Water hollows out soft limestone, then shapes and decorates the cave. It drips from the roof, splashes on the floor, shedding dissolved minerals that build up into fantastic shapes of solid stone. Stalactites hang down; stalagmites jut upwards, both 'growing' about 1cm every 100 years.

Falling thunder
A hard rock such as granite is not easily worn down by water. When a river reaches a cliff of hard rock, it crashes over, often at 150 km per hour. If you go to Niagara Falls, you will know why its name means 'thundering waters'.

ica (6,670 km)... .... highest waterfall, Angel Falls, South America (980 m)... ....

17

Canyon descent

The helicopter blades beat a rhythmic roar. 'Ready?' your pilot asks. Then, suddenly, the ground vanishes, and you plunge over the rim of the Grand Canyon. Walls of rock tower all around you. The world's greatest canyon – 1.5km deep, up to 29km across, and 349 km long – fills your whole view. Far below, the Colorado River glints in the bright sunlight.

River power

The Grand Canyon was formed entirely by the action of water. For millions of years, the Colorado River has been wearing away the soft rock to shape this spectacular gorge.

.... Grand Canyon, U.S.A., most massive canyon.......................

The Grand Canyon is so deep that it could hold four Empire State buildings, one on top of another. Descending into it, you seem to go back in time, passing layers of differently coloured rock up to 400 million years old. Bands of older grey-blue limestone and pink granite give way on the Canyon floor to heavy black rocks formed 2,000 million years ago.

Time travel
You can see fossils in many layers of the Grand Canyon. Fossils are the remains of ancient plants and animals preserved in rock. In the higher layers are reptiles, and insects like this one. Further down, you might find fossils of prehistoric sea animals.

.... Hells Canyon, U.S.A., deepest gorge (2,408 m)................................

Mountain climb

High mountains are hostile places for all life. Glaciers, or moving rivers of ice, topple frozen cliffs, split open crevasses and start avalanches. The air gets thinner the higher you go, making you gasp for breath. Thin air can cause headaches, loss of balance, double vision, even death. The temperatures are well below freezing; the wind claws at your body and frost bites into your skin. Everything is a struggle – even writing up your diary.

Climbed up glacier, wriggled across deep crevasse on a shaky snow bridge. Ice creaked and groaned. Temperature −10°C.

Headache, first sign of air getting thin. Made base camp at 5,000 m below ice cliffs. Took six weeks to adjust to effects of altitude.

Himalayan diary
Easy climb through foothills. Harder to pass rocky rubble left by melting glaciers to reach 4,000 m.

Annapurna
Himalayas
8,078 m

Vinson Massif
Antarctica
5,140 m

McKinley
Alaska Range
6,194 m

Narrow escape. Tower of ice fell, starting an avalanche. Jumped! Howling blizzard filled goggles with snow at 6,000 m.

Body ached all over. Tiring even to make hot drink, although water boils at lower temperature at this altitude. Gasping in thin air. Breathed oxygen while asleep.

Climbing with oxygen. Drove iron pin into rock. Without gloves, hands would freeze to the metal. Struggled exhausted on to peak of Everest 8,848 m up – the top of the world!

Everest
Himalayas
8,848 m

Kilimanjaro
Tanzania
5,895 m

Aconcagua
Andes
6,960 m

Mont Blanc
European Alps
4,813 m

Cook
ew Zealand
3,764 m

Eruption!

Volcanoes are mountains of fire that sit over hot spots in the Earth's interior. When they erupt, molten rock called lava makes new land. Some volcanoes erupt under the sea, piling up lava into islands. Imagine being on a volcanic island watching the stages before eruption.

April 5 Peering into the volcano's crater, you see a lake of fiery lava boiling up from inside the Earth. Hot gases rise from it.

April 26 Dry ash and cinders go pitter-pat on your umbrella. The air smells of sulphur, as the hot gases react with rocks near the crater.

May 4 The volcano rumbles. Glowing cinders and hot gravel rain down, rattling the leaves and piling up on the ground.

May 5 Molten lava pours over the crater's rim and down the slopes. When it hardens, the lava will make fertile new soil.

May 6 Deep rumbling; steam shoots from the crater. Fiery rock and lava pour out, piling up to make the mountain higher.

… Earth has 850 active volcanoes… Hawaii has the two most active, Mauna Loa and Kilauea

Volcanic islands

The Hawaiian Islands are the tips of volcanoes that erupted in the Pacific Ocean centuries ago. Tropical forests grow on the rich soil.

Steam blower

When hot rocks in the Earth heat underground water, it emerges as a spring or as a geyser. Iceland has thousands of geysers and hot springs. Old Faithful, in the U.S.A.'s Yellowstone National Park, is the most predictable geyser. It blows, on average, once every hour. Bacteria and simple algae are the only forms of life than can live in scalding hot springs.

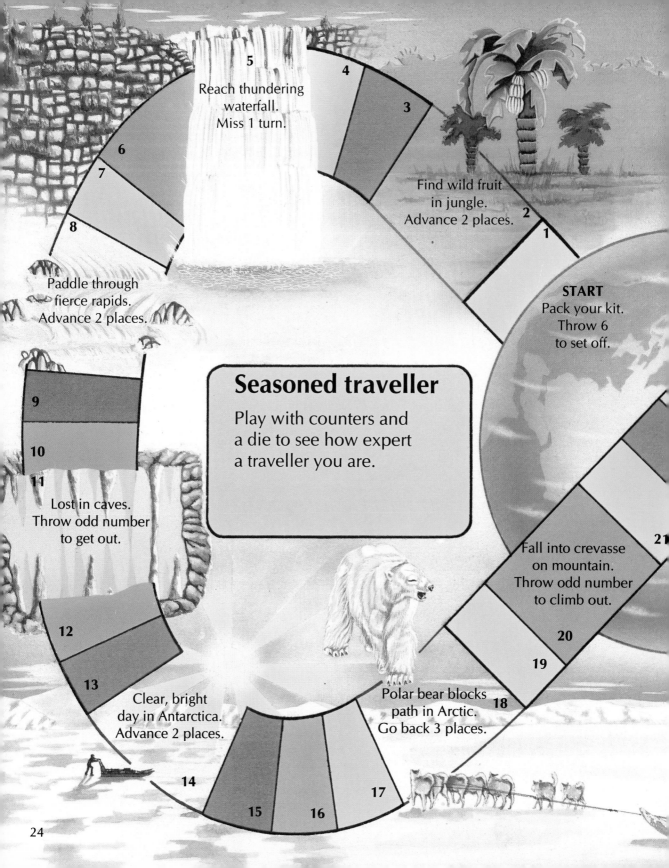

5 Reach thundering waterfall. Miss 1 turn.

4

3

6

7

8

Find wild fruit in jungle. Advance 2 places.

2

1

START Pack your kit. Throw 6 to set off.

Paddle through fierce rapids. Advance 2 places.

Seasoned traveller

Play with counters and a die to see how expert a traveller you are.

9

10

11

Lost in caves. Throw odd number to get out.

Fall into crevasse on mountain. Throw odd number to climb out.

21

20

19

12

13

18

Clear, bright day in Antarctica. Advance 2 places.

Polar bear blocks path in Arctic. Go back 3 places.

14

15

16

17

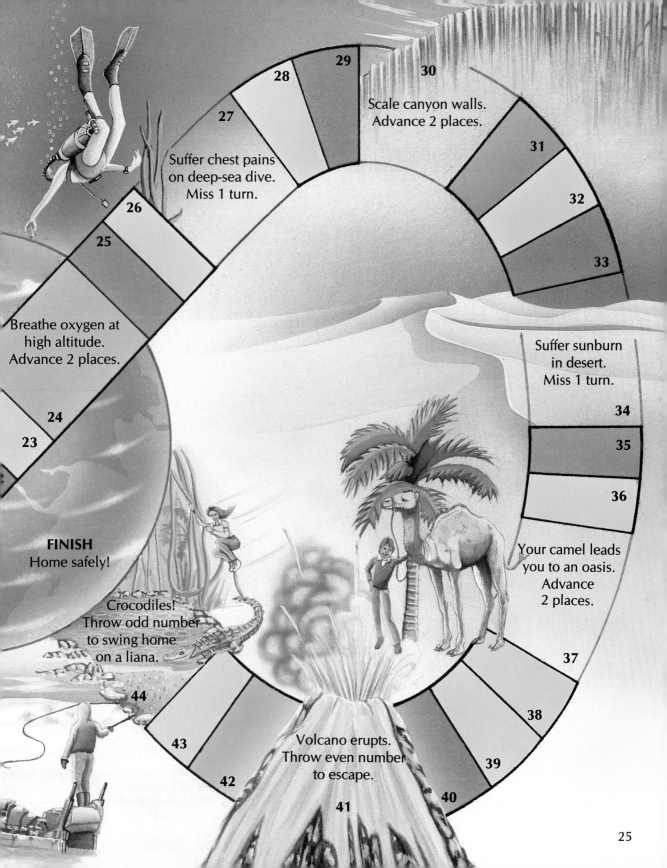

28

29

30
Scale canyon walls.
Advance 2 places.

27
Suffer chest pains
on deep-sea dive.
Miss 1 turn.

31

32

33

26

25

Breathe oxygen at
high altitude.
Advance 2 places.

Suffer sunburn
in desert.
Miss 1 turn.

34

35

36

24

23

FINISH
Home safely!

Your camel leads
you to an oasis.
Advance
2 places.

Crocodiles!
Throw odd number
to swing home
on a liana.

44

43

42

Volcano erupts.
Throw even number
to escape.

41

37

38

39

40

Spot the difference

Compare the Earth that you have just explored, with other planets and their moons in our solar system. There *are* similarities. But Earth is the only place that has water in liquid form, clouds full of rain, hail and snow, blue sky, and an atmosphere that supports life: plants and animals and humans. Find the clue in each scene that tells you it is a picture of the Earth.

The surface of Mars is red and dusty. What tells you this is an Australian desert?

Clue A flowering Desert Pea.

This is the Fish River Canyon in Namibia, Africa. How do you know it isn't the huge canyon on Mars?

Clue The river.

There are mountains on Mercury. This is Mont Blanc, France. How can you tell it is on Earth?

Clue The snow.

What tells you that this is Antarctica, and not Europa, an icy moon that orbits Jupiter?

Clue The blue sky.

There are craters on our Moon. This is Arizona Crater in the U.S.A. How do you know it is on Earth?

Clue It is raining

Venus is covered in thick clouds. What tells you that these are clouds over the Earth?

Clue The aeroplane's shadow.

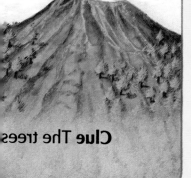

...o, another moon of Jupiter, has active volcanoes. How do you know this is a volcano on Earth?

Clue The trees

This is a rock from South Africa. What tells you it isn't one of the rocks that orbit Saturn?

Clue A fossil footprint.

Lightning flashes deep in Jupiter's atmosphere of poison gases. How do you know this is Earth-lightning?

Clue The bird.

The incredible journey

Crunch! Ring! Your spade breaks the soil, your pick strikes stones. You are tunnelling to the centre of the Earth, where no one has ever been before. Drilling 4km down now, as deep as the deepest mine, you begin to feel very hot. It's 55°C, the rocks are hot to touch. You bring down a futuristic machine to plough into the mantle of rock and liquid metal. At 2,000 km, the thermometer inside super-mole reads 3,000°C. Can you survive the next layer, the outer core? It's mainly liquid iron and nickel, and about 3,900°C! If you do, you will reach the solid inner core, and so solve the mystery of what is really at the centre of the Earth.

.... Earth's crust 25km thick................. mantle 2,900 km thick.........................

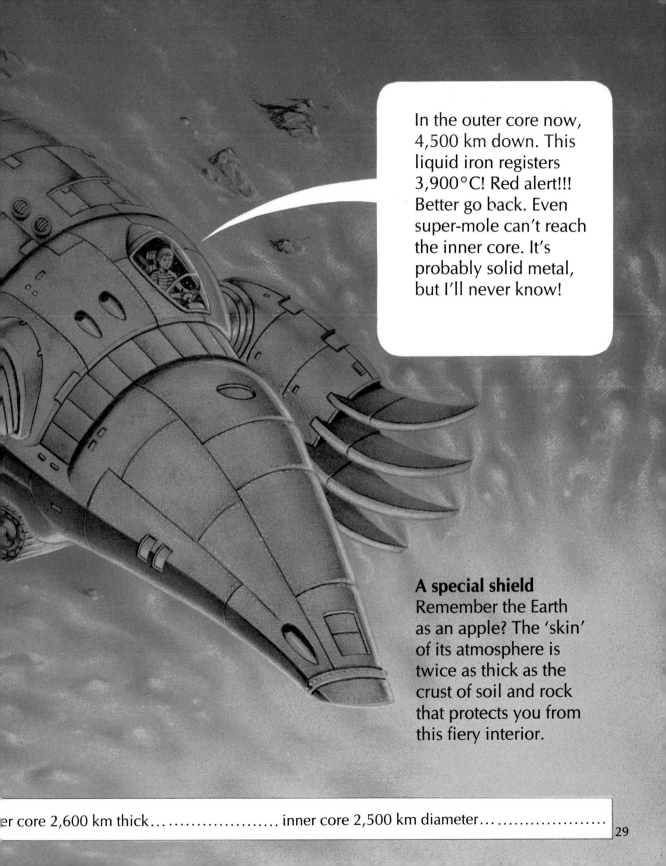

In the outer core now, 4,500 km down. This liquid iron registers 3,900°C! Red alert!!! Better go back. Even super-mole can't reach the inner core. It's probably solid metal, but I'll never know!

A special shield
Remember the Earth as an apple? The 'skin' of its atmosphere is twice as thick as the crust of soil and rock that protects you from this fiery interior.

er core 2,600 km thick..................... inner core 2,500 km diameter.....................

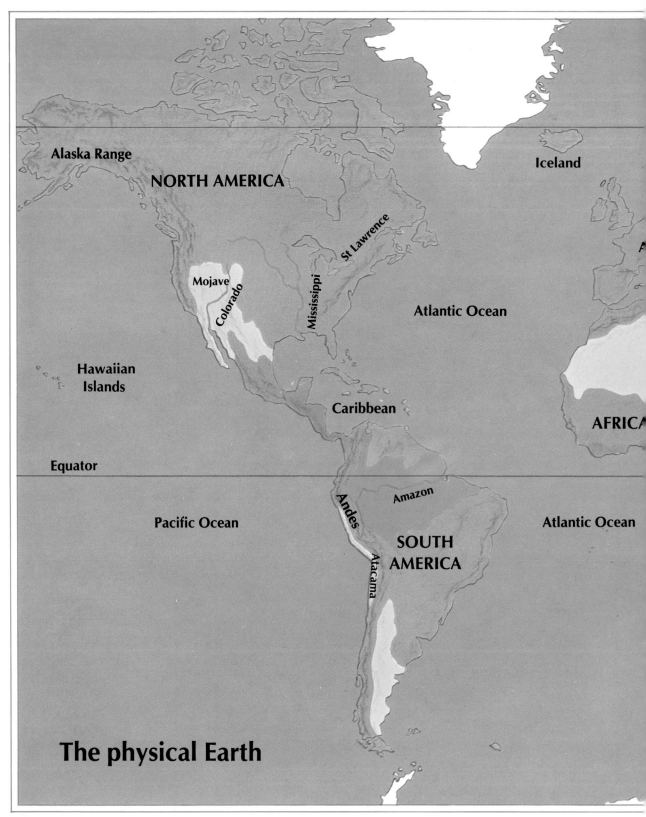

Alaska Range

Iceland

NORTH AMERICA

Mojave

Colorado

St Lawrence

Mississippi

Atlantic Ocean

Hawaiian
Islands

AFRICA

Caribbean

Equator

Andes

Amazon

SOUTH
AMERICA

Pacific Ocean

Atacama

Atlantic Ocean

The physical Earth